THE
PROSPERITY
PROJECT

THE PROSPERITY PROJECT

BUILDING ABUNDANCE AND A MAP FOR A LIFE WELL LIVED

JOHN LOHRENZ

MERACK

johnlohrenz.com

Published and distributed by Merack Publishing

Library of Congress Control Number: 2020921132
Lohrenz, John, *The Prosperity Project: Building Abundance and A Map for A Life Well Lived*

Paperback: ISBN 978-1-949635-47-8
eBook: ISBN 978-1-949635-48-5
Hardcover: ISBN 978-1-949635-49-2

DEDICATION

I would like to dedicate this book to
my family who I love dearly!

EJ, Mom and Dad, Wayne and Holly, and Blue

EJ is my daughter and she changed everything in life and still does! Always for the better. She is my best friend and keeps me young and vibrant as I try to keep up with her energy, love, and incredible consciousness. We are always on the journey side-by-side!

Mom and Dad are the incredible dynamic duo of wisdom, love, and entertainment! If you are lucky enough to be their friend, love and laughter is inevitable. They have a life well lived and continue to inspire me and make memories I will always cherish! They are the best mom and dad you could ask for!

My brother Wayne and I have a special relationship I treasure greatly. I witnessed when both Wayne and my daughter came into this world (the only two people on earth I've had that experience with) and we share an incredible closeness and I love them dearly. They are both difficult to teach but somehow I have been able to do it!! Haha. Holly you are an angel and thank you for everything you do!

My dog Blue is the ultimate companion for loyalty and laughter. This shows you true prosperity for $80 at the Rancho Coastal Humane Society provides a lot more kicks than a dinner bill!

Family is everything to me! They have made my journey so rich and I thank and love them for the prosperity they bring to my life.

CONTENTS

INTRODUCTION

"HAPPINESS IS THE MEANING AND
PURPOSE OF LIFE, THE WHOLE AIM AND
END OF HUMAN EXISTENCE."

ARISTOTLE

Life is a giant game of whack-a-mole. Just when one part of your life is in alignment, the monster pops up in another.

There are so many books on the market that are trying to get you to live your best life. But what does that really mean? *What is that? How do I define that? And how do I do that?*

The problem with most books on this topic is they are a one-size-fits-all definition of treasure that may well have nothing to do with what *your* definition of prosperity looks like. Wouldn't it be so much easier if someone taught you how to build a map to *your* treasure?

I have experienced a classic midlife crisis of epic proportions and made a comeback. I had to dig deep and give my all to come back from the last rung on the ladder to hell. My recovery, renovation, and relaunch was accomplished with self-discovery, research, conscious thought and effort, and determination. Shaking off divorce, joint pain and replacements, alcohol, pain meds, obesity, and the brutal bottom big D—depression. Through all of that I found my formula for true prosperity and want to share it with you here.

This book is a passion for me as it is inspired by my life up to this point and all that I have seen, experienced and researched. I have been on Wall Street for over twenty-five years and dealt with thousands of families and their wealth—not to mention a bunch of the things that go along with it (sons and daughters with addictions, chronic illnesses and disease, divorce, and even death). Being positioned as a trusted advisor in a family's life ended up making me a trusted advisor on so much more than just a family's finances. Together we saw the dot-com bubble grow—and burst—in the late 1990s and early 2000s. Then we weathered the financial crisis in 2008-2009. If that wasn't enough, we then had the COVID-19 pandemic to deal with. Navigating wild swings in the markets and the economy, while being a confidante for families and their wealth, has been invaluable for learning life lessons on everything to do with prosperity and loved ones. I have seen the good, the bad, and the ugly.

This book delivers a proven formula for you to define what *your* personal meaning of prosperity truly is. By the end, you'll have a well-defined map to navigate your life's best effort! It's a project. And this project becomes your PURPOSE. And it is through living out your purpose, day in and day out, that at the end of your life you'll feel as though it's been a life well lived. You only have one shot at this world, so stop saying "someday" and get started right now! **We always hear that we need purpose in our life and if living our best life isn't a purpose, what is?**

Success in any discipline requires two non-negotiable components that are proven to work every time:

1. Inspirational and motivational tools that are repeatable and sustainable.

2. Technical formulation and execution of a game plan you are accountable for.

No one from the happiness sweepstakes is going to ring your doorbell and whisk you off the couch to Happyville! Life is a chronic stress marathon. It's going to be there in one way, shape or form, no matter what (there's that whack-a-mole thing again). But it's something that can be conquered with the right organizational thought processes, motivation, and a formula you can follow daily for yourself and your family.

When you evaluate success and winners, you will find that there are those that get lucky and win a single championship or have a great year or two in business. However, dynasties of six world championships or thirty years of great business results are the mark of a proven formula for success followed religiously and then repeated. Tom Brady, Jack Welch, Warren Buffett, Oprah Winfrey, and Coach Steve Fisher and Brian Dutcher of SDSU all exemplify what it takes at a core level of grit and determination, coupled with intelligent thought and planning, and fierce, consistent execution.

The Prosperity Project dives into the pillars of Health, Wealth, Relationships, Growth, Adventure, and Legacy. The background of this discipline is solidly anchored in the history of human achievement, modern psychology, thought leadership as well as personal trial and error. Financial planning and analytics have been the structural basis of my daily profession for the past twenty-six years, and have given the concepts in this book a solid foundation on which to build the framework and blueprint for your Prosperity Project map.

It transfers to a much-bigger calling of true prosperity beyond the assets in the portfolio or in the estate.

> "The ultimate source of happiness is within us. Not money, not power, not status. Some of my friends are billionaires but they are very unhappy people. We must look inside."
> The Dalai Lama, *The Book of Joy*

No matter where we find ourselves in life, we can always seek better! Striving for that serenity, and the feeling we have this "all figured out"—at least on the baseline of daily gratitude and a life well lived—is a noble journey. Living with a formula that forces us to have purpose and direction daily works from every level of our humanness. Conscious but not cautious! Living life with a vigor and vitality created through health and wealth we've created is priceless!

If your life was a movie, would you want to watch it? Are you a superhero or a comeback story? How does your script look for the rest of your life? Would you fall asleep watching your life movie? How does it end? Are you consciously and intelligently planning and managing your life of prosperity?

Join me on the journey of self-discovery! Lets escape this reality of the masses and create our unique and refined prosperous life!

PART ONE

THE
FOUNDATION

CHAPTER 1

THE PYRAMID OF PROSPERITY

"EVERYBODY WANTS TO BE RICH. EVERYBODY WANTS TO
BE FIT. EVERYBODY WANTS TO BE HAPPY."

NAVAL RAVIKANT

Living the good life! It's what we all work so hard to achieve. We all want prosperity.

Prosperity. It's a word laden with subjective bias. It may mean something different to each one of us. When I say the word "prosperity," some of you may immediately conjure the image of money. Others think of "abundance" or "luxury." And some of you may equate it with the word "happiness." For the purpose of this book, let's start by agreeing on a common definition. To me, prosperity encompasses all of the above: wealth, physical and mental health, and so much more. To be truly prosperous, every aspect of your life must be aligned. Prosperity is a holistic word—in that, one cannot be truly happy if the people around you are not well, or if one aspect of your life is in the gutter. For example, if you are living in abundance, with financial security and luxurious surroundings, but you and your wife are fighting and talking about divorce, can you truly claim that you are prosperous? If you are healthy and wealthy but alone, are you living in prosperity?

To design the formula for the Prosperity Project, I combined my professional and personal experiences and observations, with the science of psychology, health, wellness, and finance. My career and personal life have forced me to dig deeply into these fundamental human truths about how we find abundance, control, and joy in our lives. I've worked with firms who have spent billions of dollars researching the financial and psychological aspects of planning and investing for clients' futures. My personal journey has led me through education and experience in holistic health practices, financial analytics and planning, psychological research and practice. This has given me a unique perspective on the ups and downs we all face in our quest for a life well lived. It turns out, at our core, we are all the same in so many ways when we look at how our minds, spirits, and bodies function and yet, we are so vastly different in our preferences for much of what life has to offer. That is what makes our experiences so interesting and exciting and why the Prosperity Project is about YOU, what you control and how you shape YOUR life using the guiding principles of this book.

The goal of the project is to find what makes you happy and fulfilled in your life and to design an actionable plan that allows you to live that way consistently. The big question is of course, *where do I even start?* It makes sense to begin with the science of happiness. What makes us feel joy and fulfillment? Finding the common ground of how we think, act, and feel is a great place to start and this led me to the research of Abraham Maslow. His landmark work on human motivation in his 1954 book titled *Motivation and Personality* outlined our "Hierarchy of Needs," a concept that remains a very popular framework in sociology research, management training, and secondary and higher psychology instruction.

Maslow's original Hierarchy of Needs states that lower levels must be completely satisfied before moving to higher pursuits. Today, scholars prefer to think of these levels as continuously overlapping each other. This means lower levels may take precedence over higher levels at any time. When we speak of lower levels we are talking in terms of the basics we all need to be happy. Food, shelter, income, sex, healthcare and relationships are at Maslow's first two levels. When we don't have these in full alignment, we have anxiety and stress levels that don't allow us to go to higher levels of joy, therefore these must be handled first.

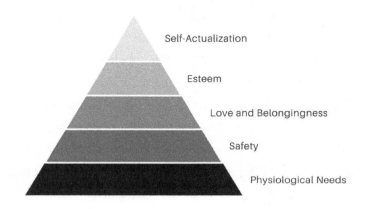

Using Maslow's basic formula and combining it with scientifically backed research, financial planning knowledge, and holistic health principles, I developed what I now call the Pyramid of Prosperity. You will immediately notice that just as it is true for Maslow's Hierarchy of Needs, we focus heavily on the basics in our Pyramid of Prosperity. Transferring Maslow's work from the 1950s to present day, I have built the Pyramid of Prosperity to reflect our basic fundamental truths for happiness in today's world. To me it's a common sense approach to stand on the shoulders of giants in building my own formula.

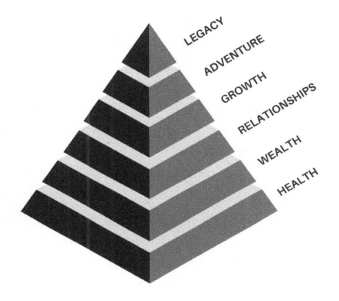

First and foremost, at the base of the pyramid is our health. Without it we have nothing. Regardless of your riches, you will not be happy if you are unhealthy. Second is our financial security. If you are worried about your money lasting for the rest of your life, you will not be consistently happy at your core. We must cover our basic living expenses securely before moving on. The third layer of the pyramid is relationships. We must get this part of our life straight or we will struggle to find happiness. We've all heard the common saying, "happy wife, happy life." The concept works both ways and holds true at work, in your home, and out in your community. If you have people who upset you constantly, you will always end up with a pit in your stomach and that is a horrible way to live. Work must be done to set boundaries or get rid of toxic relationships in order for us to find our path to happiness.

Health, wealth, and relationships are the base of your Pyramid of Prosperity and what I refer to as The Big Three. They are the core foundation we use for our map to prosperity and peace in our lives. Daily attention, with intentional effort, is required to get this right. These three are common to all of us and are scientifically proven requirements to live a conscious and fulfilling life.

Moving up from the base, we dive into the areas where we start to find more differences in our approach and preferences. Growth, adventure, and our legacies are where we paint our canvas with creativity, fun, and our own unique perspectives on life. This is where we really have a good time!

These principles are very evident in my daily practice of working with families. Whether they are clients I have known for twenty-five years or people I meet for the first time, these fundamental needs hold true across the board. When people are healthy, financially secure, and have good relationships, they have a lot more fun and are living the good life!

They are able to plan their adventures for travel, find new ways to grow, spend time planning activities with family and friends and envision how their legacy will play out. They are living vibrant and conscious lives doing the things that bring a sense of purpose and vitality! Focusing daily on what is important may not have been a formal plan but it is what they naturally find themselves doing and it becomes a habit. I have learned a great deal by observing and interacting with successful and happy people. This book is about sharing the attributes and habits that are common to these types of people in the Pyramid of Prosperity.

Finishing the last three levels of the pyramid are growth, adventure, and legacy and they provide the passion in daily living. Regardless of the path you choose for your growth, the important thing is you consciously make the plan and put the effort in daily. Adventures are the spice in your life—whether it is a local adventure like hiking to a new trail or a picnic in a new park, or something much grander like a Costa Rican vacation or skiing the Swiss Alps—giving yourself something to look forward to is critical to your well being. Whatever gets your heart beating and keeps your dreams alive, adventure is something we should all spend more time planning.

Legacy is how you will be remembered by loved ones and the community. It's not just about the money or things, it's about your stories, wisdom, and keepsakes as well. Carefully think this out and it will bring you joy in your life by helping others!

Now it is time to build your formula, as we move forward, we will cover all the levels of the pyramid in detail to help you create your unique plan. There will be the basic core that you need to pay attention to daily and incrementally improve. The Big Three require work and attention or they will erode and rust. Consistently caring for these and holding yourself accountable will give you a sense of control and certainty in your future. It frees your soul to explore the finer things in life! It's time to put it all together and plan for the good life of joy and prosperity!

CHAPTER 2

THE FUNDAMENTALS

This book isn't meant to tell you what to do or how to live. I only want to provide suggestions, observations and lessons I have learned from my own life, from my client's lives and from the research I have done. The formula I will provide is a map, however, it is only a starting point. I fully expect you to tweak it, mould it, and color it in a way that best suits your style. Whatever floats your boat, or so they say. We are all diverse characters and no two maps will look the same. I am simply here to act as a guide and help you keep some important information in mind as you go forth and plan for your present life and future happiness.

In order for this book to have maximum impact on your daily lives, I felt it was important to first talk about the fundamentals to any successful plan. **Every year America provides us with the data from the social experiment called New Year's resolutions. It is an epic failure as a whole and shows why just simply setting goals does not work. Eighty percent of the people who set New Year's resolutions have failed by the start of February! Only eight percent make it to the end of the year. The question is why? What is going on to lead to this high level of failure?**

As you begin your journey, I need you to know that it isn't always going to be easy. This isn't something that you can wrap up in one month, or even in a year. It's definitely NOT a New Year's resolution. It's about creating a plan that will last you the rest of your days, allowing you to live a life of happiness and joy. I would be remiss to set you loose on the project without giving you the key tools needed to make sure that you can be successful in this endeavour.

Preparation

John Wooden won ten National Championship titles at UCLA from 1964 to 1975 and was the first person inducted into the basketball hall of fame as a player and a coach. He was widely respected for his ability to teach the fundamentals of basketball and life to his players, and was loved deeply by such former players as Hall of Famer Bill Walton. Each year, when his new recruits arrived at their first practice, Wooden did not start with high level discussions of strategy or complex drills—he didn't even start with layups. He made these highly prized superstars learn to tie their shoes the right way. Pull up your socks leaving no loose flaps inside your sneakers. Pull the laces tightly and evenly then tie them tighter.

This was done so players wouldn't get blisters, costing them valuable practice time or, worse yet, spraining an ankle because they were lazy putting on their shoes. All this to say, we need to know the fundamentals of preparation, planning, and execution or we will have a very hard time achieving what we set out to do. This also applies to your Prosperity Project.

Purpose & Planning

With a clear purpose we can set the right goals and make a consciously well-thought-out map to create our journey to our most meaningful life. When you pursue your purpose, your life becomes filled with direction and meaning and the key is to identify what is important to you!

Purpose is unique to each of us and it really is important to prioritize the areas you want to work on daily. Health, wealth, and relationships are critical for our happiness and having a daily game plan for all three really helps us to feel less stress and to be more productive. It gives us the feeling of progress and self satisfaction that our efforts are moving us closer to our treasure on the map. Once we have clearly identified what it is we want to accomplish in these areas we can make a plan.

Don't stress now about making a plan, that is the reason for this book and what I am going to navigate with you in the chapters ahead. I've built the formula so that you just need to do the work on a personal front, inserting into the plan what is right for you. Just be aware that having a plan to guide you through the rough waters is an absolute must.

Execution

I had the good fortune of meeting John Lynch, GM of the San Francisco 49ers, and former great all-pro safety in the NFL. (All-Pro is an honor bestowed upon professional American football players that designates the best player at each position during a given season.) We were at a men's meeting in Rancho Santa Fe, California, and I asked him what the difference was between an all-pro player and one who had a less successful career. He replied that of course you find athletes who can jump higher and run faster but that is not what the real difference is. *It's that the great players stack their solid effort days back to back to back* before *having a letdown. They don't allow themselves to be "off" for an extended period of time. When they do have an off day, or cheat on their program they limit the streak to just one day. They get right back up and on to their formula for success.* You need to do the same with this Prosperity Project—if you fall off the proverbial wagon, dust yourself off and get back on there.

If living your best and most prosperous life isn't the greatest goal you have ever put on the table, I don't know what possibly is! So let's do this right from the beginning and take the time to build your formula.

Repeat, Repeat, Repeat

Small, incremental changes on a daily basis will lead to lifelong habits that require less conscious thought and effort. By following the formula that I've designed, you'll begin to incorporate these habits into your daily routine and over time they become natural. You'll get into the zone where happiness, abundance and prosperity are a fundamental part of who you are, and you'll be able to share those lessons with others you care about.

The Importance of The Big Three

We are going to start with The Big Three as the fundamentals of prosperity. These must be done right or we have no shot at success. The basis for our happiness depends on them being in good order—they do not have to be perfect but there must be purpose-driven initiatives happening almost daily. Even the conscious effort for improvement will give us the fuel we need and optimism that provides us the peace of knowing we are going where we need to go to feel prosperous. While there are chapters in this book that focus on the top half of the pyramid, they can be considered "the nice to haves", things that will make your life better than you ever dreamed it could be. However, The Big Three are the "need to haves." It's imperative you get them right. Let's take a high-level look at each of the three and how they should factor into your day-to-day living. We will dive deeper into each layer in subsequent chapters.

THE BIG THREE

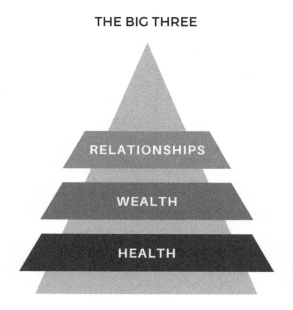

Health

Health is by far the most important factor in your life. It is an absolute and the only proof you need is your memory of the last time you were very sick. Our sole focus when we are lying sick in bed is wanting to feel like we're back to normal and we would give nearly anything for that. In order to have the mental, emotional and physical capacity to work towards prosperity, we need to have our health in order.

Wealth

The saying goes money can't buy happiness but you go ahead and try being happy without it. I can tell you it won't go well and I am not Nostradamus! Money isn't everything but it is a close second to oxygen if you are broke. My experience with clients and friends over the last thirty years has really brought to my attention a glaring difference between people and their relationship with money. By far, the happiest and most balanced are those who don't have to worry about money or are able to make sure that they are in the right place with their mindset that they don't worry about it.

Relationships

It's important to focus on cultivating meaningful relationships in our lives. When we are truly mindful of living well, we want our family and friends to be on the top of our list of priorities. It's so important we have harmony with those who are a part of our daily lives. There can't be constant stress or discomfort with those whom we spend the majority of our time. Work and home are imperative.

We need other people in order to thrive! Loneliness is one of the leading causes of depression, anxiety and premature old age. You need someone to share your adventures with, someone to laugh with, and someone to cry with. You need a community of people to create new memories with and to reminisce about old stories. A happy life is a shared experience. This book is meant to provoke your thoughts about the status of your relationships. Who is your support system? Who are the people that bring you joy? Are you purposeful and proactive in growing and maintaining relationships with them? What can you do to be more involved in groups and communities of people you enjoy?

This is something we need to consciously have a game plan for, and to execute our actions to be close to people and communities.

Health + Wealth + Relationships = Baseline Prosperity

CHAPTER 3

HEALTH

"OUR BODIES ARE OUR GARDENS,
OUR WILLS ARE OUR GARDENERS"

WILLIAM SHAKESPEARE

Health is the foundational layer in the Pyramid of Prosperity for good reason: it is the only thing that you are guaranteed to have with you for the rest of your life—for better or for worse. Our health affects everything we do, from the way we think, eat, and sleep, to our view of ourselves, others, and the world. Conversely, each of those things have a great effect on the state of our physical and mental well-being.

Think of all the amazing things you are able to do thanks to good health. Whether it is exercising, traveling, and working or even just sitting and enjoying time with your family without pain—most people don't realize how fortunate they are to have their health until it is compromised, and at that point it can sometimes be too late. It's crucial that we practice gratitude for our bodies and minds and what they accomplish for us each day. Our quality of life is precious and we do not want to mess it up if at all possible.

After years of observing the health and wellness of my friends, family and clients, what really stands out to me is the vast differences there can be between two people at the same stage in life. One may be able to go fishing in Alaska at age eighty-five, while the other can't go for a walk alone at age seventy.

Just sit with this for a minute and recall how the aging process has affected you and those around you. Think about the differences you see in the quality of people's lives and their lifestyle. This is not meant to be judgmental, but a learning experience for self-awareness and personal growth. Maybe it is your Mom and Dad, Aunt or Uncle, Grandparents or family friends. Think of those who are living vibrant lives and how they are able to move and groove at a later stage in life versus those that cannot. *Consider what the differences may have been in getting them to that point. Was it a poor diet? Smoking? Alcohol consumption? Lack of exercise? Did they handle stress poorly?* What was it that led them to age more quickly and lose their vitality earlier? You want as many good years as you can get on this planet and it's startling to see how a healthy lifestyle can impact the last twenty years of your life.

I have a friend who owns one of the largest RV dealerships in the country with locations all over the US. One day we were talking about how he sold RVs to people in his prime demographic—sixty to seventy years old. He took a ruler that was eight and a half inches and placed his thumb at the six and a half inch mark. He then put it up close to my face to get a good look. He said that the ruler represents our life expectancy and where his thumb is, is how long you have lived now at sixty-five years old. That two inches is all you have left. Don't you think you should buy a motorhome soon? Look at how much time you have to go. Whoa! It will make you think! This is why we need to really treasure our time as we move through life. It is never too late to improve our health.

If there is a pulse there is hope!

What we put in our bodies and how we move is so critical to our longevity and quality of life. How we handle and process stress is critical to the release of toxins, inflammation and our mental health. We need tools and strategies to make sure we do this to the best of our abilities while balancing our current enjoyment in life with the long-term outcomes. Sometimes we have to forgo the immediate gratifications and look at the big picture. It's the same as what we must do with our money. If we spend it all too early, our bank account is empty, and that is what happens to our health as well.

When we were younger, in our twenties and thirties— blessed with youth and vigor—we could easily overcome our sins. (And didn't we take *that* for granted!) After a period of being inactive, our bodies would recover after a few weeks of intense working out. If we ate junk food or drank too much, we'd simply clean up our acts and feel better relatively quickly. As we get older, our bodies don't recover as quickly from abuse or slovenly behaviour. It becomes harder to stand up, more difficult to walk, more challenging to sleep well. So, we sit more, living a life of boredom and inactivity. The more we sit, the unhealthier we become, both mentally and physically. As depression and cardiovascular disease set in, we wonder if it is still reversible. If we are lucky, we may be able to recover from some of the damage, however, many of us are not so blessed. It's such a shame because most of this misery is preventable. Let's turn this around while we can and get the most out of our health and life!

My Mom is a shining example of how lifestyle decisions can impact us at a later stage of life—she is living the absolute dream of an eighty-three year old and she earned it! She moves without pain, walks five to ten miles a day and plays golf at a very solid level. My mom travels the world by herself, going on safaris in Africa and pub-crawls in Ireland. Mentally, she is sharp as a razor and feisty as the day is long! She teaches quilting to students around the world and has a vast network of friends from her hobbies and life. She handles stress like a Buddhist monk!

This is why:

- She walks daily as her form of exercise
- She is conscious about what she eats and supplements her food with vitamins
- She is spiritually connected
- She limited consumption of alcohol in her life, not drinking until about age sixty (don't try and take her wine now though!)
- She is close to family and a large network of friends
- She has financial security
- She will be remembered fondly by a very long list of people (if she doesn't outlive everyone)

My mom is living the Pyramid of Prosperity and her story is one we should keep in mind as we dive into the nitty-gritty of the reality many North Americans are facing when it comes to their health.

Even with all of those positives, my mom still talks about the struggle to keep her weight where she wants it—no journey is perfect and the rewards don't come without challenges. This is something that I constantly have to work on and it's likely that you will too. Don't let that deter you from making the changes you need to make!

The Blue Zones

I recently read Dan Buettner's study of the Blue Zones, an investigation into the lifestyles of centurions, or elderly people over 100 years of age. There are five regions (Blue Zones) around the world: Sardinia, Italy, Okinawa, Japan, Loma Linda, California, Nicoya Peninsula, Costa Rica, and The Greek Island of Ikaria. All five of these areas boast incredibly high percentages of centurions, and Dan Buettner and his team were intrigued. They wondered what elements factored into such astonishing longevity. Though these cities were from vastly different areas of the world (with some in Asia, Europe, and one in North America), scientists found each culture held some common denominators. These centurions live healthy, full and vibrant lives and are valued members of their society. Some of the common attributes included:

Move Naturally

While most of these seniors in the blue zones are not running five miles a day or doing push-ups, they are gardening, walking and even riding bikes. They are walking up and down stairs, getting up and down from sitting on the floor, and they intentionally move their bodies each and every day. It doesn't need to be complicated. Find something you love to do and is sustainable. If you feel like you're being tortured by your choice of exercise, it's not going to last and you're going to feel stressed every time you think about having to get on that treadmill, or jump on your spin bike. That's why New Year's resolutions only last an average of one month because burnout causes failure. Find the form of exercise that invigorates you and draws you back time and again.

How often do you hear people talk about getting in their ten thousand steps per day? There is a reason that has become such a common theme and it's because walking works! It gets us out into nature and it's low impact so our joints don't go through a huge recovery process. It's free, it's easy to scale to your level—add a hill climb in there to challenge yourself—and it's social so grab a friend or your dog and get out there!

I highly recommend that you add a simple ten minute stretch in your morning routine to age backwards.

Stretching allows us to remain functionally strong and healthy and it reduces pain. Whether you are an athlete, a surfer, a skier or a mom who needs to haul groceries and kids in and out of the car, keeping your body limber and flexible is going to enhance your daily life.

There should be a component of strength and resistance training to keep your muscles working as they should. Strong bodies mean fewer injuries. You want to remain strong as you move into your later years so you can travel and be active in your daily life.

Eat Wisely

In the blue zone regions, they are not strictly vegetarian eaters, however the amount of red meat they consume is substantially less than we do in North America on average. In addition, they eat naturally—food that comes from the earth. Processed foods are reduced or eliminated wherever possible in these regions. My home state of California has one of these blue zones in Loma Linda, and their focus on plant-based and whole food diets is evident in the research. This concept isn't foreign, it's doable and is taking place right here in America.

Let's be honest here: we're not all trying to win a beauty pageant or run a triathlon. We're looking to maintain a reasonable weight that allows us to move our bodies and feel confident in our clothes. We want to keep an eye on our long-term health concerns and we know that being overweight is a major factor in aging, chronic illnesses and even premature death.

The great news is that this is not a thirty day project, this is a lifestyle change that will benefit you daily for the rest of your life! Making small, incremental changes to your physical health and wellness will allow you to do the things you love for a much longer period of time. We all know that we need to eat more fruits and veggies, we should probably ease off of the wine (we can't party like Keith Richards if we want to be scaling mountains at seventy!) and perhaps we need more exercise, but it doesn't need to be complicated.

WEIGHT LOSS
(Our Biggest Challenge)

Losing weight, it's a really big pain in the ass! There is just no other way to say it. The statistics show that this is overwhelmingly the biggest health challenge we face in America[1]. Over two-thirds of us are considered overweight

---

1   https://www.niddk.nih.gov/health-information/health-statistics/overweight-obesity

or obese and the impact this has on our physical and mental health is enormous.

I have battled with weight loss for the entire second half of my life. I was thirty years old when my daughter was born and I clearly remember feeling like I was the one who had been pregnant! I was carrying fifteen extra pounds—and that was only the beginning of what was to come. Every year that went by saw me adding another pound or two, which didn't seem like a big deal until one day I stepped on the scale to see 274 pounds and 40% body fat staring back at me. It was a rude awakening that left me wondering what had happened and how I had let it get to this.

What followed was honestly one of the toughest mountains to climb in my personal wellness project. My Mom's story of her own struggles with weight left me with the sense that it would always be a fight, but it was a battle I knew I needed to take on for my overall happiness. I have finally lost the weight after going through ups and downs for three decades. Having my Prosperity Project Map as a guide to fall back on when the struggle intensified has been vital to my success.

Right Outlook

This is the absolute key to life! In order to have any chance at true prosperity, you need to have your mental health rock solid—or at least be striving for improvement. **Your thoughts and how you shape them are going to determine who you are, how you act/react, how the day works for you or against you, and whether or not you achieve your life's goals and dreams.**

We all need to stop spending unnecessary time on our phones, computers, and watching the news on TV. We are being negatively influenced by "big data engineers" that screw with our minds for money! Do a digital detox and see how much better you feel.

The folks in the blue zone regions have a purpose, a reason to get up every morning. They find meaningful ways to spend their time.

Handling your stress and anxiety is critical to maintaining the right outlook. Becoming mindful is what this is all about and I recommend reading the book *The Untethered Soul* by Michael Singer as a powerful starting point. Studies have shown mindfulness can truly change the outlook and health of people who practice a few simple strategies on a regular basis. Lower stress, better sleep, reduced pain, and improved immunity have been shown to be the results of a mindful meditation and gratitude practice.

This can be as simple as just sitting and breathing deeply for a minute or two with your eyes closed a couple times a day. Don't have contempt without investigation and make it out to be something only done by some weirdos wearing robes and ringing handbells. It is a powerful way for all of us to quiet our minds and slow down the flow of meaningless self chatter.

The gratitude you practice can be in your own thoughts or you can write things in a journal as often as daily, weekly, monthly or whenever you feel funky in your days and need a jump start out of stressville.

The top sources of gratitude in the US are:

- Our families
- The freedoms we have in America
- Good health
- Close friends
- Objects we own like a new TV or old truck we love

Between our busy lives and big causes of stress, who can blame us for having gratitude deficit disorder, a term coined by Robert Emmons who is the author of *Gratitude Works!*

Emmons states, "When people are grateful they feel more alert and alive." He goes on to say, "it strengthens relationships and the benefits can be felt almost immediately."

Take the time to do a regular practice of gratitude in your life as often as possible and you will notice a difference. It replaces the space you might be using in your day for negative chatter.

Social networks

All of these centurions actively seek human connection. They are members of clubs, associations, or churches. They eat dinner with their children and play with their grandchildren. They chat with their neighbors and say hello to strangers. Human connection is, after all, the anecdote to loneliness. We will dive further into the importance of relationships in a later chapter, but know that having those connections is key to a strong mental outlook.

This study (www.bluezones.com) seemed to articulate and validate everything I have spent the last years of my life pondering. It dovetails and supports The Pyramid of Prosperity. I didn't just make this stuff up: people all over the world are living long, happy and fulfilling lives by following a tried, tested and true formula.

SUGGESTIONS FOR PHYSICAL AND MENTAL HEALTH

- Meditate everyday for a specific amount of time.

- Write in a Gratitude Journal.

- Read self-development books that dive into the importance of differentiating between your subconscious and conscious mind:

  - *The Power of Now* by Eckhart Tolle
  - *The Untethered Soul* by Michael A. Singer

- Be present! Have a "Mindful Morning" routine that allows you to be present with yourself—no screens, no spouse, no kids! Just ten minutes with you (and your coffee).

- Move your body every day.

It's important to be accountable for this plan. Use a daily checklist to keep you focused on the key areas that we discussed above. If you are currently trying to accomplish a goal—such as tracking what weight you are at and what your target is—a checklist will consistently keep you on track. By making sure that you are writing down your gratitudes and implementing the "Mindful Morning" routine, you'll notice a shift in your daily sense of happiness and overall well being. You can visit johnlohrenz.com to download your copy of the checklist.

YOUR HEALTH CONTEMPLATION:
Use this space to make note of the things that came to mind regarding your personal health as you read the chapter above!

CHAPTER 4

WEALTH

"MONEY IS ONLY A TOOL. IT WILL TAKE YOU
WHEREVER YOU WISH BUT IT WILL NOT
REPLACE YOU AS THE DRIVER."

AYN RAND

Have you ever really sat with yourself and asked the question, *what is the meaning of money to my happiness?* Our financial assets and income certainly play a role in our perception of joy and factor heavily in our quest for happiness. As the numbers fluctuate on our bank account statements, our sense of security also rises and falls, and fear creeps in. Will we have enough saved to last us our lifetime? Will we be able to take that trip, or buy that car? And if we can't, will we still feel fulfilled and successful?

These questions are at the center of what drives us emotionally around assets and money and our quest for feeling prosperous. The relationship we have psychologically with our money has everything to do with our happiness! **Finding the feeling of safety, security, and surety of the future is truly what we all strive for as healthy, functional people.**

Knowing that we are covered for our shelter, food, utilities, medical care, and necessities in the modern world is critical, regardless of our station in life. The needs are as unique as humans are themselves—some are very content with a little and some need to have as much as possible to think they are happy. A person who has millions is no different in how their perceptions, fears and actual emotions affect their happiness if they feel like the mansion, yacht, and country club membership may be in danger. They won't get much sympathy, but it creates the same sense of inner turmoil as the person who needs a place to live, or food to eat. Whether we are early in our career or moving into retirement, the need for security and safety are the same. The difference is that in our early years we are building our wealth and earning money, and in our later years, we are relying on what we have saved. Let's take a look at how that plays out.

0-25 Years of Age: We are born with no assets and without the help of mom and dad, we don't have much during the first twenty-five years of our life. This time period is about education and exploration. We are trying to find ourselves a vision without hurting ourselves through our lack of wisdom and youthful zest for adventure!

25-55 Years of Age: Life gets very complicated and busy. We now start our "real life" with careers, families, plans for retirement, and aging parents. As all that is going on, we do our best to enjoy our lives while earning an income and saving for the future.

55-65 Years of Age: It is here where we seriously begin to figure out how we are going to live out our golden years and enjoy life to the fullest. Planning is key. Assets should be repositioned in a way that provides safety and security for our base level of income required to meet our expenses while also investing for growth and future adventures.

65-90 Years of Age: Enjoying the ride! Grandkids, travel, hobbies, nature, friends, family—all the best of life! Staying fit and healthy and grooving is critical to the length and quality of this period of our lives!

90+ Years of Age: Smiling and reminiscing on a life well lived!

Building Wealth

Time is really the greatest single concept for our understanding of growing abundance! Einstein pointed this out when he stated that "the power of compound interest is the most powerful force in the universe."

Whether you are buying stocks, real estate, art, collectibles, a 401k, or building a business, TIME is your most critical factor for success. Statistically speaking the longer you have, the better for the growth of an asset.

BUILDING ABUNDANCE AND THE POWER OF TIME!

One of the best recent success stories has been investing in the stock of Apple. We are all familiar with the story, we can see how it played out when we take a look around: whether at the restaurant, grocery store, or even at the beach, people are on their iPhones. This investment has been incredible and an example of how a bit of luck and time can build abundance in a big way! $10,000 invested in January of 2000 is now worth $1,554,220. I have clients who were fortunate to buy and hold Apple stock for this period of time and it has changed the course of their retirement futures.

Apple is an extraordinary story and not something you can put into a plan for retirement and count on it happening. There is a lot of luck involved to hit a home run of that magnitude but we can always be striving to have a part of our investment portfolio looking for great growth opportunities.

A long-term example of how a little can become a lot is the Gracie Groner story.

In 1931, Grace Groner was a young, resourceful woman who got herself a job working as a secretary. (That's what it was called in those days.) After three years working at Abbott Labs, she bought three shares in the company's stock at $60 per share. As her shares grew, Grace continued to live a modest life and kept re-investing her dividends. By the time Grace passed away, at 100 years old, thanks to stock splits, re-investment and appreciation, she had turned her original investment of $180 into a seven million dollar fortune.

At a young age, Grace understood some key concepts: invest early, allow time to work for you, protect your assets, and live within your means. Though she could have cashed in and lived a life of luxury, Grace chose to re-invest, creating a reliable source of income that lasted the rest of her natural life. It even allowed her to leave a legacy. Upon her death, she left nearly all of her estate to her alma mater, Lake Forest College, allowing nearly 1300 students to pursue opportunities they may never have had otherwise.

It is great to look at success stories that show it is never too late! I love the story of Colonel Sanders and the Kentucky Fried Chicken franchise. Harland David Sanders was a classic character. He held a number of different jobs throughout his life including steam engine stoker, insurance salesman, and filling station operator before he started selling fried chicken from his roadside Kentucky restaurant during the Great Depression. He developed his secret recipe and his patented method of cooking chicken in a pressure fryer. He opened his first franchise restaurant in South Salt Lake, Utah in 1952 at the age of sixty-one. He had a rapid expansion of the franchise across the United States that was overwhelming for Sanders and in 1964 at seventy-three years old, he cashed in. He sold the company for $2 million ($16.5 million in today's dollars.) He retained control of operations in Canada and was paid as the brand ambassador for Kentucky Fried Chicken. This just shows that it is never too late to make it all happen for your own personal prosperity success story and that the stock market is not the only game in town!!!

Enjoying the Results

When a person is preparing to retire, there is a shift in strategy from growing their assets to creating a steady income stream to live on for the rest of their lives. This is a drastic change in mindset.

In my opinion, the amount of money you have is not nearly as important as your ability to manage your wealth effectively. Someone with twenty million dollars in the bank is no better off than someone with two million if they don't have a healthy relationship with money. In fact, I believe you can be even worse off with twenty million if you are spending it unwisely. Spending without a clear plan will bring nothing but stress and anxiety, as you wear your financial situation down brick by brick. You can easily burn through your savings if you aren't careful, and may wake up one day wondering where it all went. This is why it is crucial to examine your *emotional* relationship with your bank account.

Like it or not, understanding your sources of income, following a budget and sticking to the plan is what will determine the quality of your retirement. You absolutely cannot bury your head in the sand when it comes to your finances. Having a defined path and a plan of action will offer you peace of mind knowing that your basic expenses will be covered. Trusting your basic needs will be met in the years to come is what allows you to sleep well at night—it's emotional freedom.

The most laid-back person I know is a guy named Bob that I often run into at the beach. He is always down there with his dog in the morning and is completely carefree about every discussion. He could care less about the stock market or really anything in the economy. When I asked him why, he told me he has everything paid for and his income is highly predictable at a level he is content with, so he doesn't mess around with it. He has rentals in the real estate market, some tax free bonds, a small assortment of blue chip stocks, and a nice cushion of cash in the bank. This is the ideal situation of having an income stream that matches expenses with as much safety as possible. No greed and no reaching for too much. The stocks don't have anything to do with him paying his bills or giving him anxiety about his lifestyle. They are long-term investments for maintaining his buying power of aspirational and fun goals for the rest of his life.

This is a concept I use extensively even though Bob doesn't know it. It is a concept called Floor Income Planning. This is rooted in the fundamentals of the world of finance as a safety-first philosophy and discipline. It really helps to break down your overall strategy and cuts through the painful jargon. There is an endless amount of information on what the best investment strategies, lowest fees, and who the most caring institutions are when it comes to your retirement. Trust me, it comes down once again to you! You are the one who will be there at the end with your hand on the wheel of your ship, navigating your journey. Start with the end in mind of you being happy, secure, and confident in your financial life. Once you get the basic framework built, you can deal with the details. That is why we use the planning that has the lowest amount of risk and stress as the starting point. Once you can establish your base level and meet those fundamental human needs so you feel secure, you will really feel like you have climbed the mountain.

A Floor Income plan matches up your predictable sources of recurring income with your base level of recurring expenses and allows you to know two things:

1. You are covered for the basics of shelter, food, utilities, and medical expenses for life.

2. The sources are as safe, secure, and predictable as possible.

Your Floor Income lays the foundation for your whole Prosperity Project Plan. It needs to be steadfast and strong, and retain the ability to weather unforeseen changes in markets and politics. If your foundation isn't sturdy and you cannot pay your monthly bills, all other layers of

The Pyramid of Prosperity will collapse. You cannot have adventures if the heating bill remains unpaid. You cannot leave a legacy if there is no food in your cupboards.

Essentially, your Floor Income should consist of a portfolio that remains consistent, reliable and untouched. I've always said, "A portfolio is like a bar of soap. The more you touch it, the smaller it gets." Once we satisfy the basic needs the fun begins.

> Having a concrete financial plan that provides the monthly income to take care of our bills for the rest of our lives is one of the most liberating feelings!

Once you have this established you are able to invest the rest of your money into areas that will be focused on growth and enrichment. You can dive deeper into the Floor Income plan at jklwealth.com.

The stress and worry about money is only a part of the equation and the variables you can control around it are vast and wide. I see drastic shifts in how someone's outlook on life changes when there is a major transition. *Divorce and death are two of the biggest and most stressful events in our lives. Planning for the aftermath and having a secure grasp on the future is really important when these life-changing events occur.* They really highlight and amplify the benefits of having it all put together nicely in an easy to understand plan.

Allow me to share two snapshots of clients of mine—women who were financially smart and were able to rise above adversity. The first is the story of my friend, Evelyn. I share this to illustrate the importance of your Floor Income as a buffer against disaster. The second snapshot is of my friend, Julie. Her story will demonstrate the wisdom of living within your financial means.

EVELYN
DON'T SWEAT THE SMALL STUFF

When Evelyn came to me in the late-1990s, she was looking forward to her impending retirement. Together, we planned a Floor Income, which would afford her $50,000-60,000 annually (a substantial amount of money at that time). When the recession hit in 2008, Evelyn's investment portfolio took a hit, just as everyone else's did. However, the difference was, her Floor Income was not impacted. Despite the economic instability of the time, she was still able to pay her bills. Granted, she had to slow down on her adventures for a while, but when the market eventually recovered, she was free to play once again. The fact that she had built a consistent, dependable income gave her confidence, knowing that her daily survival would be unaffected by market fluctuations.

JULIE
WEALTH WISDOM

My dear friend Julie's world was shattered when her husband suddenly died of a heart attack. At the time of Jim's death, he and Julie lived in a gorgeous California house, with a luxurious pool and more square footage than they needed. Suddenly responsible for this mortgage and all of their expenses, Julie was losing sleep and worrying deeply about her retirement. She knew she would have to invest aggressively in order to cover her basic expenses and understood the unpredictable and unforgiving nature of the stock market. It was too much uncertainty for her to stomach.

It was clear, she needed a plan that would allow her to enjoy life and not worry about her investments. Julie made the brave choice to reduce her living expenses so that she could be comfortable within her financial means. She decided to leave the expensive California lifestyle and trade it in for a simpler life in Tennessee. Julie now lives in a new custom home on a golf course. Despite having cut her living expenses by over 60%, Julie is living with more joy than ever, golfing, traveling and saving money.

Once you have created an accurate financial picture and have built a solid Floor Income, your retirement could very well be saved from catastrophe. Both Evelyn and Julie understood this and were able to go on and live vibrant lives. They not only met their basic needs, but were able to thrive, have fun and experience true prosperity.

True prosperity lies in what I refer to as Aspirational Income. This is the money that allows you to have those adventures, be playful, enjoy hobbies, travel, be philanthropic and create legacy. Your Aspirational Income will be at the root of your Retirement Manifesto.

Your Retirement Manifesto is the fun part. It's the part where you get to sit back and dream about what you want your life to look like. We know happiness is not about money. Money can afford us comfort and help us sleep better at night, but it's not what gives us purpose or makes us feel fulfilled. So, the question becomes: *what makes you happy?*

Do you want to spend your winters in Hawaii? Go on an African safari? Have an annual family gathering?

What's on your bucket list? Learn to play an instrument? Ride a motorcycle? Jump out of an airplane? Visit all the continents? Dream big! But, don't forget to think about the fine print as well.

Even more important than the events that happen on occasion, take a moment to think about your daily life. What would you like it to look like? Do you want to live somewhere with an ocean view? Care to buy a small farm and plant garlic? Do you wish to hike in the mountains each morning? Who would you like to spend your time with? What would you like to spend your time doing? Along with your financial plan, you should be creating a vision of your future life that accounts for your physical, spiritual and emotional health as well. Your Retirement Manifesto serves as a road map to a great, holistic life. It gives you a purpose to lean on and a plan to follow.

> ### YOUR WEALTH CONTEMPLATION:
> Use this space to make note of the things that came to mind regarding your personal wealth as you read the chapter above!

CHAPTER 5

RELATIONSHIPS

"THEY SAY MARRIAGES ARE MADE IN HEAVEN,
BUT SO IS THUNDER AND LIGHTNING."

CLINT EASTWOOD

There is so much influence on our happiness from the relationships we have in our lives that it's one of the Big Three for daily reflection and attention on our journey. This is a top priority to put considerable time, thought, and effort into if we want to truly live our best life! I will always treasure my close family, friends, and clients and keep them at a high priority. The joy I receive from my relationship with those closest to me can't be duplicated with the purchase of a new shiny object or anything I can consume.

Rafting, surfing, going to the beach, or just simply eating a meal together with my beautiful daughter are my best days! My almost daily conversations with Mom and Dad and my close friends keep a smile on my face. These human interactions are critical to my personal prosperity. Texting or emailing won't get it done for me. I need a live heartbeat and voice for it to be a top shelf interaction!

Just as fabulous relationships are so uplifting there is the other side of the coin. We all have people who can become difficult in our lives. It is very important to our journey and our feelings of joy that we stay vigilant in managing both the good and the bad when it comes to our relationships. We really have to take a step back when we realize we are stressed out too often by someone in our lives. The two hotspots are at home and at work. If you are having difficulty with your marriage or partnership at home, and it is a constant dramatic episode of toxicity, you can forget about being happy until it is on the right path. It's the same with a relationship in your daily work. If someone is triggering you frequently, you must find a way to either set boundaries and manage your emotions or move away from the relationship.

The bottom line—relationships are just like our health and wealth, we must recognize how critical they are to our well being and put in the work to make them as rich and enjoyable as possible!

Take the time to organize your thoughts about your relationships. I use two categories for positive or negative relationships in every aspect of my life. They are either Code Red Contacts or Lifesuckers. Sometimes they crossover but most of the time they are consistent in how they make me feel.

Code Red Contacts

Code Red Contacts are those people in your life that are positive and uplifting influences you can count on to celebrate your wins or pick you up when you are down from a loss. They are those who make you feel good after you talk to them and spend time with them. They always seem to make you smile. It's these people you want to identify, and these relationships where you should put in the work to nurture them to their fullest.

This should be done with conscious and thoughtful effort and planning. Make your list of Code Red Contacts and make the effort to call them and see them regularly! Make an annual trip out of these important people in your life!

Pick up the phone and talk to one of them every single day as part of your Prosperity Project.

It takes a lot of work to build that bond and maintain it for a period of meaningful time. That being said, I have friends where we have such a strong foundation that we may not talk or see each other for long periods of time, and when we do it's right back to the good times as if we were never apart! Those are magic!

My dad was an oilfield truck driver. He owned his own company, moving and servicing drilling rigs. This meant he was on call day and night, working 24/7—but he loved it. His job became his purpose and his employees became an extension of our family. He enjoyed connecting with people at work, shooting the breeze, learning about their personal lives and seeing the same faces day in and day out. My dad's business became an enormous piece of his life and he formed relationships that have lasted him through his retirement years. People who worked for him have gone on to do great things in their lives and it gives him great pride and joy to keep in touch with them and see how well they are doing. There is a group called The Wildcatters, men who were successful in the oil field over decades—tough, hardcore guys who met the same challenges in life and share a common bond. Having that connection for my dad is enormously valuable. They talk on the phone regularly, look forward to seeing each other in person and they are the definition of Code Red Contacts.

Life Suckers

On the flip side of your Code Red Contacts, we have the Lifesuckers. It's fairly self-explanatory what these people do. Eliminate those interactions and relationships that constantly bring you down. This is easier said than done— but you must do the work on this to find the daily baseline of peace and happiness from which you operate. Do an inventory of Lifesuckers and define your relationship—is it one that you can remove entirely, or do you need to find a way to manage it? Plan your way forward to either making it better, or eliminating the problem. The higher the personal involvement and commitment level, the messier and more difficult this is. However, the happiness you will experience once you have made those necessary changes will shine so bright you will wonder why you waited so long to do it!

The Power of Relationships

Relationships are crucial for long-term happiness. Companionship and belonging are basic human needs! If we don't become proactive in our efforts to connect with others, the risks for depression and loneliness are high.[2]

While a strong social support structure is linked with lower rates of depression, the opposite also holds true. The more isolated you become, the more at risk you are to having depressive feelings. Simply said, loneliness seems to be a large contributor to depression and the antidote lies in the quality of our relationships.

The Blue Zones study dedicates three of its "Power 9" lifestyle habits to social connection, stating that having a sense of belonging can add up to fourteen years to your life expectancy. That's a substantial number. Developing a sense of community is good for you on so many levels.

First of all, it provides you with a sense of purpose, a reason to get your butt out of bed in the morning. If you know people are waiting for you, or you are looking forward to spending time with someone that day, it's hard to feel lonely and depressed.

---

2 Segel-Karpas, D., Ayalon, L. and Lachman, M.E.(2018). Loneliness and depressive symptoms: the moderating role of the transition into retirement. Routledge: Aging and Mental Health. 22(1), 135-140.

Secondly, being around a group of like-minded people helps you develop good habits. It's been said that you are the sum of the five people you spend the most time with. Just as loneliness, depression, and anxiety are contagious, so is laughter, healthy habits, and the desire to live life to its fullest.

Thirdly, having a strong tribe of friends and family will ensure there are people to care for you when you are down, mentally or physically. We can't do life on our own. We all need a helping hand from time to time and it's comforting to know people who've got your back.

When you are working, relationships are formed with ease, out of simple proximity and common interest. Networks are organically built through staff meetings, email exchanges, and phone calls. You might bump into a co-worker in the hallway and stop for a quick chat. In retirement, your daily access to other humans may be somewhat restricted unless you intentionally create opportunities to be around them. At first, the amount of effort required may seem daunting. You might feel unmotivated to reach out, to go out, or to organize a trip for the sake of visiting family. Don't let that stop you because you need to consider the alternative. Staying in your house will only leave you feeling lonely, neglected, forgotten and depressed. So, instead of waiting for people to come to you, be proactive and put yourself out there!

It may be a good idea to begin by making a list of possibilities for the cultivation of social networks. What areas of your life may afford social connection? Take stock of your current hobbies and ask yourself, "What is my relationship with…?"

- My family
- My friends
- Clubs
- Associations
- Community groups
- Spiritual gatherings

If you find that your list is markedly short, that's okay. There's lots of room for improvement! Most communities offer a myriad of opportunities for social connection. However, it involves you getting off of the couch and leaving your house. Ask yourself what services are available in your community or which common interest groups you could possibly join. For example, you could:

- Volunteer at your local school, church or community group
- Take a cooking class or an art class
- Look for community projects such as building a playground, or local environmental clean up

- Organize a block party for your neighborhood
- Join a book club
- Join a choir or music group
- Take a class at the university

If, at this moment, this feels way outside of your comfort zone, that's okay. You can start small. Keep in mind that not all relationships need to be so formal. Perhaps you could begin by saying hello to the gentleman you see at the dog park each morning. Greet your neighbor and invite them to go for a coffee. Chat with someone in line at the grocery store. All of these little interactions add up, making you feel seen, heard and valued on a daily basis. I like to treat every new person I encounter like it might be my new best friend. By making conversation, I make room for the possibility of a new relationship. Yeah, it might feel strange at first, but being friendly is similar to exercising a muscle. The more you do it, the easier it becomes. There is nothing worse than spending your days isolated and alone, feeling invisible, like a ghost of your former self. Stepping outside of your home, even for twenty minutes a day, will make a difference in the quality of your life.

One of the hidden gifts that came from our experience with COVID-19 was that the value of human connection and relationships became undeniably evident. As we spent weeks and months nestled in our homes, avoiding unnecessary contact with the outside world, society began to get creative in the collective desire for connection. It was a beautiful thing, really. All of a sudden, simple acts we had previously taken for granted—a hug, a handshake, a pat on the back—were taken from us and we immediately understood their value. It was a global wake-up call—we need people.

I suppose my parting advice for you on relationships is this:

1. Be proactive in seeking out human connection. Don't wait for people to reach out to you. Call them, visit them and create opportunities to be together.

2. Widen your social network by joining community events and groups.

3. Have standing dates for phone calls, FaceTime chats, and dinner with friends or family.

4. Look for opportunities to meet and greet new people. Walk through your day with your head up and a smile on your face. Say hello to strangers. Make small talk.

5. Get off your couch and out of your house! You cannot nurture relationships by watching TV.

6. Quality over quantity. Invest time and effort into relationships that build you up. And keep those who pull you down on the fringe.

7. Plan trips to go and see those people you truly love.

8. Don't wait. Start today.

YOUR RELATIONSHIPS CONTEMPLATION:
Use this space to make note of the things that came to mind regarding your personal relationships as you read the chapter above!

PART TWO

THE
GOOD
STUFF

CHAPTER 6

GROWTH

"BE NOT AFRAID OF GROWING SLOWLY,
BE AFRAID OF STANDING STILL."

CHINESE PROVERB

Growth begins the second you decide you want to grow!

2014 was not a great time in my life. In fact, I could more accurately refer to it as "dark." I was overweight, unhealthy, unmotivated, lonely and questioning my purpose. Nothing made sense to me anymore: my health, my marriage, or my happiness. Instead of diving deep and examining my fears, I chose to avoid them—and bury them, actually, under a thick layer of depression. Some might say I was in a slump, although it felt more like a cavernous hole.

I was in the darkness, at the bottom of the ocean, where all light and life are non-existent, and the weight of the seas was crushing me. I was trapped in chronic physical and emotional pain and couldn't find my way out. The daily grind was pure survival, absent of hope, vitality or enthusiasm. It took the death of a very close friend to help me move towards the surface and break through the black waters for a life-sustaining gulp of air.

Death has a knack for immediately shifting our perspectives, doesn't it? Where I was previously shadowed in the darkness of my pain, now a spotlight shone on my priorities—my health, my relationships and my purpose. These are the things that are truly important. Death was the lighthouse that lit the path to my recovery. It sounds dramatic, but it was true. My friend left a wife and children behind, a legacy of love and commitment. If I died in that moment, what would I leave? The good news was that I realized my troubles were correctable and the damage I had caused could be repaired—as long as I was willing to put in the effort. I needed to work towards becoming a better man. I needed to make a choice to either sink into the depths of depression's ocean, or swim towards my life.

Let's talk about choice. To me, there is nothing worse than complacency. If you are stranded in the middle of the ocean and you choose not to paddle, the wind will push you around. You have given up all control and will end up in a place you don't like or never thought you would be. If that's okay with you, then you have also given up every right to complain about your destination. In my opinion, if you quit, then you're done. You might as well dig your own grave on that deserted island because you have lost all will to live.

Growth comes with a certain level of personal responsibility. A high level of responsibility, actually. You *always* have control over what happens in your life. Even complacency is a choice. You are *choosing* to do nothing. You can choose to stand up and face a challenge, or you can choose to lay down and die. If the second option seems easier, if that's what floats your boat, then so be it. I did it too. For several years approaching my fiftieth birthday, I was a miserable guy because I was choosing to give up control and just let life happen, even though it was happening in a way I didn't like. I wasn't growing at all. I was giving up.

Challenges are opportunities for growth. What doesn't kill you makes you stronger, right? And, that what's 2014 was for me—my wake-up call for change. Without adversity, it would be so easy to cruise through life, never giving much thought to how we are spending our time on this earth. It was time for me to take the wheel in my own life. I had to stop being passive, simply letting things happen to me, and start being more intentional about the way I was living.

It's often said that people can't change or a tiger never changes his stripes. That is pure BS! I know I have changed dramatically in the last five years without any doubt and I have witnesses who will testify! I also know a number of people who have changed—some for the better and some for the worse. Change is always taking place, whether you are growing or deteriorating in your life.

I often think change takes place out of necessity and the catalyst may not always be predictable. There is growth often after some kind of awakening. That may be from the divorce of a spouse, the death of someone close, a brush with your own mortality, or a health issue that pops up—seemingly out of nowhere. It may just be the cumulative impact of a life you are sick and tired of being sick and tired of!

There is so much for us to experience in this world and life is just waiting for us to shake ourselves out of our rut, to brush off the complacency! Becoming a seeker who is making change is about finding inspiration, motivation, education and getting in the game.

Growth is something that comes from a much deeper place and requires original thoughts and intentions from your own mind and heart. Out of the shallow end of the pool and into the deep blue ocean of life! It does not reside on Fox or CNN. It is deeper than most of the chatter you will see on a screen.

My personal change has been due to what I guess is the proverbial midlife crisis. I had hit my inflection point and the mountain in front of me became clear. I made a conscious decision to change my life. I learned so much through this process about myself and what made me tick—it was profound. I discovered my purpose and the drive to live my best life with no looking back! I had not been able to surf for ten years, my guitar had sat dormant for way too long, my overall well-being needed a huge wake up call. My relationships needed an overhaul. My physical and mental condition was ready for a renovation. Through this process I developed the formula for change that I am sharing is this book. The results have been incredible for me and have really allowed me to live my best life.

I have gone from 274 pounds and 35% body fat to 225 pounds. I am surfing and swimming in the ocean all the time. I am playing my guitar with several other musicians and having a blast musically. The relationships in my life have flourished and business is great. My spirits are at a baseline higher than I can remember. This transformation is the foundation and genesis of the Prosperity Project.

Growth is really all about you finding a formula to take you to new heights of happiness. It is your own unique journey and completely up to you how it plays out.

My formula consists of the following:

1. I gave up alcohol and medications

2. I improved my spiritual life and purpose for personal and business life

3. I made my mental and physical health my first priority

4. I intensely focused on the relationships in my life and made changes where needed (rescuing my dog Blue)

5. I rehabilitated my mind and body to a high level for business, surfing, kayaking, hiking, fishing and music

6. I plan trips and local adventures to keep it so I'm always looking forward to something

7. I pay close attention to my legacy with my daughter Erica, and my non-profit affiliations and boards that I serve on

8. I seek out ways to improve the world and
   community I live in—like donating to clean
   up plastic in the ocean with 4Ocean and taking
   at-risk youth fishing

As you can see in that formula, I focused on each of the
foundational levels of the Pyramid of Prosperity that we've
discussed in the first half of this book. By looking at your
health, wealth, and relationships, you can begin to design
your own formula for growth. Just reading this book is
taking the first step towards change.

Building Your Formula

Growth shakes us out of autopilot mode. Have you ever
driven to the grocery store and realized, halfway there,
you cannot remember the first part of the drive? Are you
walking through the same routine, without noticing each
and every step and the joys life has to offer? I used to be
like that. I would wake up and drink my morning coffee
while watching the news, reading my emails and checking
the stock market. Then I would grab my car keys and head
out the door—often with a feeling of agitation plaguing
me. I wasn't mindful about setting the tone of my day, of
being intentional about my growth. It was coffee, news,
agitation, repeat. I would go through the rest of my day
feeling heavy and tired, wondering why I was so exhausted.

There is power in your morning routine. It can make or break your day. Making that one little change, to carefully design your morning, can alter your mood, your patience, your resilience and your outlook on life. Now, I wake up feeling light and looking forward to my day. Each morning, I enjoy 15 minutes of spiritual reading. Then I meditate, quietly focusing on my breath and centering my thoughts. Following this, I work out, moving my body and improving my physical strength. I have made sure my mind, body and soul are well cared for before I dive into my daily tasks.

What does your morning routine currently look like? How does it affect your outlook on the day ahead?

I feel the need to pause and point out that not all meditation and spirituality need be tied to religion. You don't need to be associated with a church or religious group to grow your faith. Spirituality can be defined differently for each of us. It may be having a sense of purpose, believing in something bigger than us, being in nature and having an appreciation for the natural world. Or it may simply be developing an understanding of your authentic self.

Meditation is simply a mindfulness practice, a way to quiet your mind and get in touch with who you are, at your core. Again, there are many ways to meditate, all of them equally valuable. Some people enjoy a guided meditation, some repeat a mantra, some walk silently in nature, and others like to sit in stillness or focus on their breath. The type of practice you choose to dedicate yourself to is not as important as how it makes you feel. Each of us is different and has a different relationship with spirituality. And that's great. As long as you are engaging in a regular practice that helps you block out the stress of the outside world and concentrate on your own sense of calm and grounding, then you are evolving as a human being.

I find it helpful to have a checklist of growth-minded habits, a daily action plan that holds me accountable. When life gets busy, the first things to go are usually the ones that should never be sacrificed—your self-care practices. Too many meetings today? I guess I will skip the gym. No! The gym is what keeps your stress level manageable. How about skipping tonight's episode of your favourite TV show instead?

I've always said, "What gets measured gets done." And having a checklist is a great way to measure your growth. It serves as a tangible plan for activities that will enrich your life.

Your checklist may include activities such as:

- Eating healthy
- Playing music

THE PROSPERITY PROJECT

- Arranging social engagements
- Being in nature
- Exercising
- Reading
- Spiritual practice
- Meditation

Whatever you choose to put on your list is fine, but keep in mind, it needs to contain daily routines to help you become a better, happier, and more fulfilled person.

Keeping a journal is another habit I have cultivated, one which serves multiple purposes. First of all, it helps me remember where I have been and analyze where I am now. It enables me to create a plan for the future. Where do I want to go? I can track past goals and assess my success and growth in various aspects of my life. Secondly, writing in a journal helps track my moods and find patterns based on behaviour. For example, if I have been a real beast, grouchy and irritable, I may look back on my journal to notice I haven't meditated or worked out for eight days. Now that I see the pattern, I can make a change. You might use your journal to record your bucket list, checking each activity off, once you've accomplished the adventure. You may use it as a refuge to sort through complicated emotions, a tool to find inner peace. However you choose to use it,

80

keeping a journal is an excellent method for measuring your emotional, spiritual and mental growth.

Don't overcomplicate this, any notebook will do. I want this to be approachable and straightforward so that you take action—rather than getting stuck on where to start.

Growth isn't meant to be easy. It's meant to take you places you wouldn't otherwise get to, and that can be down right difficult. But, stick with it! Having a personal consciousness about growth is what will allow you to live your life with vitality. You need to approach each day with a positive mentality. Growth fights boredom, negativity, decaying bodies and minds. **It is growth that enriches your life and inspires you to seek adventure.**

YOUR GROWTH CONTEMPLATION:
Use this space to make note of the things that came to mind regarding your personal growth as you read the chapter above!

CHAPTER 7

ADVENTURE

"IF YOU THINK ADVENTURE IS DANGEROUS,
TRY ROUTINE. IT'S LETHAL!"

PAULO COELHO

As we ascend the levels of The Pyramid of Prosperity, we finally dive into the fun stuff. How would you like to spend your days? What will make you smile? What do you have to look forward to? Enrichment activities and amazing adventures stimulate your creativity and inspiration and add an extra layer of joy and recreation to your life. This is where you get to explore your purpose. What is your reason for getting out of bed each day?

Each and every one of us—regardless of age or status—needs a purpose. Without purpose, we end up bobbing aimlessly at sea, subject to the whims of the ocean tides. This chapter is designed to help you define a meaningful lifestyle. I want you to take control of your ship.

In my opinion, true enrichment encompasses three distinct facets. To live a vibrant, happy, and prosperous life, all humans need these things:

1. Something to do
2. Someone/something to love
3. Something to look forward to

To live an enriched and meaningful life, you are required to search for joy. You need to be proactive in filling your days with activities you love and people who make you happy. You can't expect this to just *happen*. You need to *make it happen* and this calls for effort and planning. Enriching your life should be a daily venture, not something you chase once in a while. Without consistent, intentional enrichment practices, you are living a bleak existence. You are a coloring book without crayons.

Let's not over-complicate this, though. I'm not saying every day needs to be ziplining across the jungle or hiking the Grand Canyon. Enrichment comes from exploring a new section of the beach in your neighbourhood, trying a different local cafe for lunch or finding a green space that you haven't experienced where you can get outside and enjoy the benefits of nature. When you're ready to explore further, start planning for bigger adventures.

Adventure

Dreaming about an adventure has become so much easier thanks to the internet. The entire planet and all it has to offer is at your fingertips to discover and visually experience. You can plan your travel routes into the far reaches of Central America or a ski trip to the Swiss Alps with the click of a button—the only thing holding you back is your determination and motivation to make it happen.

These experiences are meant to break your routine and get you out of your comfort zone. Adventure keeps you vibrant, inquisitive and thrilled about life and possibility. Having fun keeps your mind active, inspiring curiosity and learning. It brings back a feeling of youthfulness, energy and excitement. I simply cannot stress enough the importance of planning adventure in your life.

Having special dates written on your calendar has the added benefit of providing excitement leading up to the main event. Not only do we enjoy the actual activity, but the anticipation of what's coming up brings an extra layer of joy to our days.

After months of social distancing caused by the pandemic and lockdown, I was desperately in need of an adventure! My daughter and I—along with two of my closest friends who caught wind of the idea—put a date on the calendar for an epic whitewater rafting trip in beautiful Northern California on the American River. The river has many class four rapids and is a full day of thrills. Just having this to look forward to ignited our imaginations. Our feelings and sense of well-being were drastically improved for the full month before we even stepped foot in the boat. Whether during an unprecedented time like that of COVID-19, or just in our daily lives, we thrive on the excitement that adventure brings. Stop and make a conscious effort to plan adventures—two a year at whatever price point works for you will add so much value and joy.

There is truly nothing better in life than experiencing something new, but long-standing traditions also hold a lot of value and shouldn't be discounted. My dad and I used to organize a fishing trip to Alaska each year, our annual adventure together. For us, being in nature, away from the hustle and bustle was the best way to connect. We would wake up bright and early for a coffee and then hit the water for a full day of action in the Gulf of Alaska. Though this trip was a standing annual event for us, we brought along two new people every year. It was always bittersweet, the day we left Alaska, but the knowledge that we would return the following year was enough to keep us going. And, even though I haven't been able to fish with my dad the last few years, we still enjoy our memories of those trips and chat about them often. That shared history has become woven into the fabric of our relationship.

We don't have to wait until retirement to plan adventures, nor should we. I try to encourage the younger generations to save for adventures as well. We should all be stepping outside of our comfort zones, regardless of age. My daughter, for example, is twenty-six years old (at the time of writing) and she has a long bucket list and wants to travel the world. I say, "Go for it!" What I explained to her, I will also explain to you. The joy of adventure is not limited to the days you travel. The thrill also comes from the research and planning you will do in preparation for your trip. My daughter loved researching the countries she wanted to visit, how long she might stay in each location and what kind of sightseeing may be offered. This was half the fun and kept her busy for months before she planned to depart. The mere idea of the journey sparked her imagination, gave her purpose and stimulated her excitement level. Long after she returned from her adventure, she found joy in sharing photos, videos and reliving funny stories to share with friends and loved ones. The mental health benefits of her adventure are too numerous to count.

I've said it before, and I'll say it again. If you're sitting around, you're dying. If you have nothing to do, you're decaying. If you let your body stay out of motion, after a length of time, you won't be able to get it moving again. So, don't wait around for "a more convenient time" to plan adventures. That day may never come. There will always be a reason to postpone fun. The economy is on a downward trend. The dollar isn't great. Your sister isn't well. Remember that an adventure can be big or small. If you don't have time or resources to plan a vacation at the moment, then plan a date or an event instead. The negative impacts of *not* planning adventure may convince you to become proactive in this respect.

Large adventures are easily dreamed up. Let's look at some smaller adventure ideas that will enrich your life:

- Hike a new trail

- Visit the library

- Plan a picnic at a new park

- Visit a drive-in movie theatre

- Play tourist in your own town—museums and art galleries are a great place to explore the local culture

- Find a new restaurant

- Pick up a new physical activity—sailing, tai chi, whatever intrigues you

- Seek out live music (and invite a friend to join you)

- Plan a weekend away somewhere local

- Jump in the car, put the windows down, crank your favorite music and hit the highway

YOUR ADVENTURE CONTEMPLATION:
Use this space to make note of the things that came to mind regarding your personal sense of and need for adventure as you read the chapter above!

CHAPTER 8

LEGACY

"CARVE YOUR NAME ON HEARTS, NOT
TOMBSTONES. A LEGACY IS ETCHED INTO
THE MINDS OF OTHERS AND THE STORIES
THEY SHARE ABOUT YOU."

SHANNON L. ALDER

You may have noticed a theme woven throughout this book—intentionality. The same can be said for legacy. Legacies don't just happen. They are created with careful thought and planning.

How can you leave this world a better place than you found it? How do you want people to remember you? How will you take care of those you love after you are gone?

I think the biggest misconception about the word "legacy" is that it's something that happens after you die. Your will is read, and your lawyer reveals your legacy to your family. I disagree with this way of thinking. Your legacy should begin well before you are dead and gone. In my humble opinion, you should be writing your legacy every day of your life.

Your legacy is created in the interactions you have with the people around you and the ways you choose to invest your time, and leave your estate. This is a very personal decision and it is something that deserves your close attention. Ask yourself the question, do you want to see your loved ones enjoy your lifes work and their inheritance while you are still alive? If so, do your gifting in a well thought out manner and make it the most enriching experience for yourself and your soul as you enter the later years of your life. Not everyone gets that opportunity to consciously make these plans before an unfortunate event prematurely takes them away from their loved ones, so having a plan that allows for that scenario is important as well.

The shape of your legacy is solely up to your discretion. Legacies can be philanthropic, helping communities or groups of people who need your care. Your legacy can create a social consciousness about an issue that is close to your heart. Or, your legacy can simply be taking care of those who are nearest and dearest to you.

I believe we are all inherently good people who want to make a difference in the world. Whether that world is a tight-knit circle or has a wide outreach is irrelevant, really. We all want to be remembered in a positive light and to leave this earth knowing we did our very best to take care of our people.

When you give, you help others, but you are also helping yourself. Your happiness is elevated simply by elevating something or someone else. Generosity comes back to you exponentially by giving you purpose, meaning and joy. Making a difference not only connects you to the person standing in front of you, but also to the human race as a whole. Your act of kindness matters. You matter.

Think of a time when you gave, even on a small scale. Maybe you paid for the coffee of the person behind you in line, or bought a sandwich for the homeless man on the corner. The light, airy feeling of kindness stayed with you all day, didn't it? Now, imagine that on a larger scale. Knowing your family is taken care of financially, for instance, will give you peace of mind. Volunteering your time or donating to charity adds a layer of meaningful existence to your life. Isn't the effort worth the payoff?

My friend, Shad, started an organization for people with disabilities. His life's work is the mental and physical wellness of those who have been through dramatic, life-changing events. Many had lost the use of their legs. He himself is in this position after a traumatic event in his life, so he deeply understands the feelings of loss and depression that are often present after such a drastic change. He believes in the power of physical activity, such as being on the water or out in nature. It offers a sense of freedom and independence which in turn improves mental health. Pushing 4 Independence works with other groups such as Wounded Warriors and gathers local volunteers (including myself!) who are willing and able to donate time. We have the privilege of helping others escape the confinement of their wheelchairs and the restrictions their bodies place in regular daily life. The participants get to experience a gorgeous afternoon, using specially designed paddle boards and canoes. They paddle, laugh and enjoy a few carefree hours, gliding and splashing in the water underneath the sun. It's a glorious way to spend my time and always leaves me feeling grateful for the blessings I have. By doing this once a month, I am helping Shad perpetuate his legacy as well as my own.

Let's take a minute to imagine the opposite scenario, the Mr. Scrooge version of this story. When we hoard our wealth and resources, we are left feeling lonely, insignificant and empty. Knowing we could have helped others—but chose not to—may be a difficult thing to come to terms with in our dying moments. Do you want to spend your final days counting missed opportunities and regretting selfish choices? I know you don't. So, what might be holding you back? An undefined vision? Overwhelmed by the necessary planning? Don't have the time? Concerned you may not have available money?

It's true, some legacies involve money. However, not all of us are interested in, or capable of, starting a charitable foundation. Financial legacy can be as simple as organizing your affairs so as not to leave a wake of chaos and disaster after you are gone. For many of us, this is an important aspect of life to consider. Having a Last Will and Testament is crucial, but so is handling the business of your accounts, your stocks, and your investments. Who will be the beneficiary of this planning when you are no longer around? How can your financial wealth exceed your own life expectancy and keep making a difference after you are gone? While I admit this can be an uncomfortable conversation for most, it is an important one to have. So, sit down with your family members, your lawyer and your financial advisor. Broach the tough conversation and push through this comfort barrier. You won't ever regret taking the time to create a plan that takes care of those you care for the most.

Once you have taken care of your family, you can begin to look outward and think about the impact you might like to have on a community level. The great news is, not all legacies involve money and there is never a need to deplete your pocketbook. You can be equally generous with your time, presence and efforts. For instance, a friend of mine recently noticed that his company ordered too much food for a corporate event. Instead of wastefully throwing the excess in the trash, he chose to put the leftovers in bags and gave them to homeless folks in his neighborhood. That act of kindness didn't cost him a dime, yet left him feeling great about his day.

We all want to feel as if we are here for a reason, however, our time, energy and financial resources are limited. That's why having a vision becomes so important. Instead of spreading yourself thin, I suggest you take time to decide where your priorities lie. We create effective and sustainable change when we are focused. So, take a moment to ask yourself:

1. How do you want to spend your time?

2. Which of your skills or resources can make the largest impact?

3. How would you like to invest your financial legacy?

Wealth is meant to be shared. And I'm not just referring to financial wealth, though that is also a tool to create positive change. Your wealth is in your body. You can help build houses for charity, be the one friends count on when they need to move, run a charity race and raise money for a special cause. Your wealth is in your relationships and connections. Give your time and energy to your children, your grandchildren, your neighbors and your friends. Deliver soup when they are sick, babysit the kids when busy parents need a night out, take a friend for a drink when they're having a bad day. Your wealth is in sharing adventures. Invite friends and family to picnic in the park with you, to attend a ball game or to join you on vacation.

When I leave this earth, I want to know my daughter is financially taken care of. I want her to think that I was a good dad, and did my very best to support her dreams. I want my friends to know they were important to me and remember I made my best efforts to connect with them. I want my clients to know I worked hard for their security and I cared about them deeply. I want to feel as if I gave my time and efforts, volunteering at organizations that were important to me. I want to find peace, knowing I helped my community and my family. This is my legacy.

This is the true key to happiness, the highest pinnacle of The Pyramid of Prosperity. No one can be truly happy alone, and not making a difference in the world.

I suppose it all comes down to this simple thought. How do you want to be remembered? When you die, do you want your tombstone to read: *Richest Man in the Graveyard*?

Or would you prefer the epitaph: *Left Us All Better for Having Known Him*?

> ## YOUR LEGACY CONTEMPLATION:
> Use this space to make note of the things that came to mind regarding your personal legacy as you read the chapter above!

LEGACY

CONCLUSION

There is so much joy, love, and abundance available to us when it becomes a focus and we become mindful of the journey!

The Prosperity Project doesn't contain any hidden secrets or mystical miracles that will suddenly flip the script from misery to ecstasy. However, what it does offer you is a sense of hope and the knowledge that a happier and more abundant life is right there for the taking. We simply must sync our minds and hearts and be determined to find prosperity. When we make an absolute promise to ourselves that no matter what gets in our way, we will continue our quest to be happy, nothing can stop it from happening. The path is there and we just have to draw up our map and follow it by steering our vessel on course while we enjoy the journey!

What I've shared in this book is meant to give you a high-level overview of what it will take to design a life you love. I touched briefly on different ideas that have been successful in my own journey, and provided some recommendations of where you might find personal change on each level of the pyramid. Designing your own formula based on the outline of the Pyramid of Prosperity is the name of the game in these pages. However, my greater vision for you and for The Prosperity Project is to build a community that values a life of abundance and happiness, a place where we can continue to come together beyond these pages.

I invite you to visit johnlohrenz.com. While it bears my name as the URL, it's a space that I hope you can visit to find yourself and your vision for prosperity. I want it to be a source of inspiration, motivation and connection. Where our shared stories are alive and continuing to evolve together. I've dedicated a full page to the tools that I feel are vitally important: books that I've read, websites that affect change for the better, and courses or programs that might spark interest for you on your journey. This is meant as a place of resource for you as you build out your lifelong map, and while books remain evergreen, many of my current favorite tools and recommendations are digital and ever-changing, hence my decision to have them live on my website rather than in the pages of this book.

So please, start now. You owe it to yourself to be happy, to feel fulfilled, and to create abundance in your life. Reach out, I want to remain part of your journey, to see this become a movement towards a more positive society and world.

ACKNOWLEDGEMENTS

I would like to thank my daughter Erica and office manager Rayna. These two incredible women are angels in my life and a huge inspiration for my personal transformation. They demanded I make it happen and I want to make them proud!

Mark Moniak and Scott Gates are two friends who I have had an unbelievable relationship with and who have stuck by me through thick and thin! Loyalty at its finest. If they ever even talk about writing a book I will take them out! Haha.

Randy Barry has been such a great friend and accelerant in my creative business growth and is like a psychologist working with a madman!

Jesse Iglesias is a great man and my mentor on Wall Street who was so good to me and my family! One hell of a good family man, marine, and gentleman from Hell's Kitchen.

Pops, who was the hardest working man I ever witnessed with brains, brawn, humor—a whole package of dynamite! He taught me what the real world is all about and we laugh our asses off as we go through it together.

ABOUT THE AUTHOR

John has had a long career on Wall Street, spanning over twenty-five years with major firms. The highlight of his career with Merrill Lynch was being the Manager of the Year for the U.S. in 2006. Shortly after this, he started his own firm, JKL Wealth Management, and happily continues to grow the firm while enjoying the group of families he loves working with toward prosperity.

This was quite the change from his humble beginnings in a single-wide trailer in Plentywood, Montana. Born to an oilfield truck driver and school teacher where money was scarce, he learned lessons of life that are with him to this day. The family grew up poor but his father and mother were successful as they worked their butts off and were extremely frugal with money in the early years. Though they didn't have a lot, the family was extremely close and always had food on the table. There is a fabric in those small towns of toughness, honesty, and a great sense of humor that everyone needs to survive and it is clearly ingrained in John.

He left Montana to attend San Diego State University and study finance. His selection of schools was more about bikinis than books at that age but it worked out to be an incredibly good decision and he has never left California.

John lives in Del Mar, California with his rescue dog Blue. They live the life of civilized pirates with a dose of the ocean life everyday. Blue prowls the beach every morning chasing her ball and the hobbies of choice for John are surfing, sailing, fishing, kayaking, and playing guitar (when he is away from his wealth management and book writing duties). He works together with his best friend and daughter Erica (EJ) who is twenty-six years old and works in the Tech industry. She is an athlete and Holistic Health Coach with expertise in exercise, diet, and overall health.

NOTES

NOTES

NOTES

CPSIA information can be obtained
at www.ICGtesting.com
Printed in the USA
LVHW090229100221
678883LV00011B/383